I Wonder Why
Dinosaurs

4 4935

Judy Allen and Tudor Humphries

KINGFISHER

NEW YORK

Contents

Copyright © 2008 by Kingfisher Publications Plc
KINGFISHER
Kingfisher is an imprint of Macmillan Children's Books, London.
Published in the United States by Kingfisher U.S., a division of
Holtzbrinck Publishing Holdings, Limited Partnership,
175 Fifth Avenue, New York, New York 10010.
All rights reserved.

Distributed in Canada by H. B. Fenn and Company Ltd.

Library of Congress Cataloging-in-Publication Data
Allen, Judy.
  I wonder why flip the flaps dinosaurs / Judy Allen.—1st ed.
    p. cm.
  Includes index.
1. Dinosaurs—Juvenile literature. I. Title.
  QE861.5.A42 2008
  567.9—dc22

ISBN: 978-0-7534-6221-8

Consultant: Michael J. Benton, Department of Earth Sciences, University of Bristol, U.K.

Kingfisher books are available for special promotions and premiums.
For details contact: Director of Special Markets, Holtzbrinck Publishers.

First Hardback American Edition April 2008
Printed in China

10 9 8 7 6 5 4 3 2 1

1TR/1207/LFG/UNTD/140MA/C

How to say dinosaur names

Allosaurus "al-oh-saw-russ"
Ankylosaurus "an-kie-loh-saw-russ"
Archaeopteryx "ark-ee-opt-er-ix"
Avimimus "ah-vee-meem-us"
Brachiosaurus "brak-ee-oh-saw-russ"
Ceratosaurus "keh-rat-oh-saw-russ"
Compsognathus "komp-sog-nath-us"
Diplodocus "di-plod-oh-kuss"
Dromaeosaur "drom-ee-oh-saw-russ"
Edmontosaurus "ed-mon-toe-saw-russ"
Gallimimus "gal-lee-meem-us"
Iguanodon "ig-wha-noh-don"
Maiasaura "my-ah-saw-rah"
Mamenchisaurus "mah-men-chi-saw-russ"
Parasaurolophus "pa-ra-saw-rol-off-us"
Polacanthus "pol-ah-kan-thus"
Protoceratops "pro-toe-serra-tops"
Psittacosaurus "sit-ak-oh-saw-russ"
Stegoceras "ste-gos-er-as"
Stegosaurus "steg-oh-saw-russ"
Struthiomimus "struth-ee-oh-meem-us"
Triceratops "try-serra-tops"
Tyrannosaurus rex "tie-ran-oh-saw-russ rex"
Velociraptor "vel-oss-ee-rap-tor"

3

When did the dinosaurs live?

Dinosaurs lived a long time ago—farther back in time than any of us can imagine. They were here before there were any horses or dogs or cats. They were here before there were any people.

Tyrannosaurus rex

1. Why are they
called dinosaurs?

2. Are lizards dinosaurs?

3. Were there a lot of
different dinosaurs?

lizard

Tyrannosaurus rex chasing the lizard

1. The word "dinosaur" means "terrible lizard."

2. No. Lizards are different from dinosaurs. A lizard's legs spread out sideways, but a dinosaur's legs go straight down.

3. Yes. Some walked on two legs, and some walked on four. There were small ones, big ones, spiky ones, smooth ones, scaly ones, and some with hair or feathers.

Some types of dinosaurs

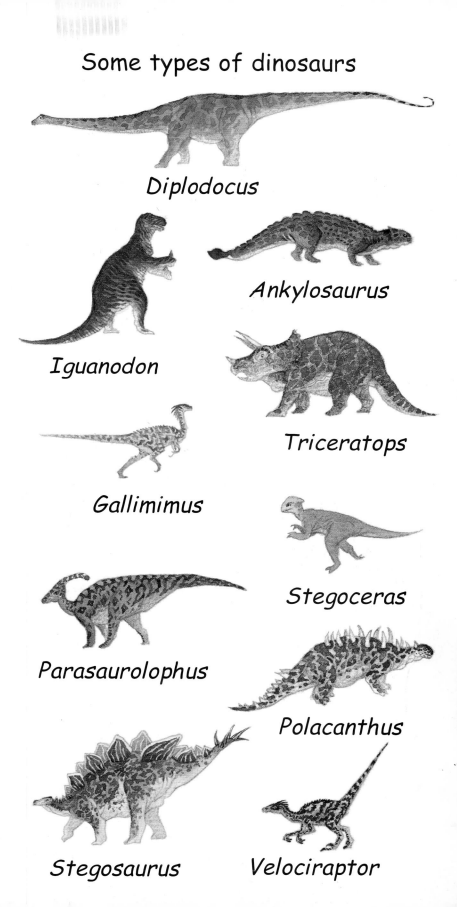

Diplodocus

Ankylosaurus

Iguanodon

Triceratops

Gallimimus

Stegoceras

Parasaurolophus

Polacanthus

Stegosaurus

Velociraptor

Food

Dinosaurs ate plants or meat or both—just like animals do today. The plant eaters ate roots, the leaves of plants and trees, and fruit. The meat eaters ate the plant eaters and each other.

Protoceratops, a plant eater, eating leaves

1. Did they climb trees
to eat leaves?

2. Did dinosaurs
eat grass?

3. How did they catch
each other to eat?

Velociraptor, a meat eater, pouncing on *Protoceratops*

1. No. Dinosaurs that ate from the treetops had very long necks.

2. No. Grass did not exist when the dinosaurs were alive.

3. Meat eaters hunted other dinosaurs. Some hunted alone, and others hunted in packs. They were very fierce.

Mamenchisaurus eating from a treetop

Fighting back

Plant-eating dinosaurs were hunted by meat eaters, so some of them had body armor. They had horns, spikes, or tails like whips to help fight off attacks. Some lived in big groups in order to protect each other.

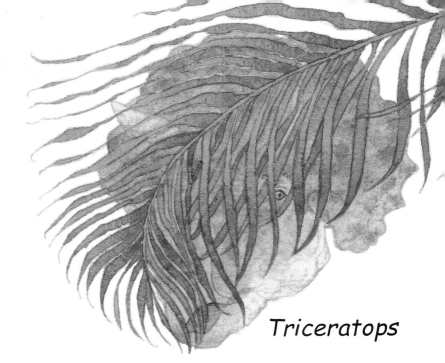

Triceratops

Diplodocus
under attack

Ceratosaurus

1. What kind of armor did *Triceratops* have on its head?

2. Where did *Stegosaurus* have its spikes?

3. Why did *Diplodocus* use its tail as a whip?

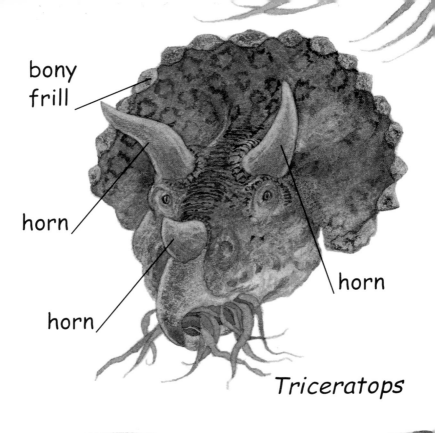

bony
frill

horn

horn

horn

Triceratops

1. *Triceratops* had hard and bony frills around its neck. It also had three horns on its head.

2. *Stegosaurus* had four spikes on the end of its tail and some spikes on its back. It could lash out with its spiky tail.

3. *Diplodocus* could use its long tail to whip attackers and knock them down.

Stegosaurus senses danger . . .

turns its back . . .

and swings its tail!

Ceratosaurus
knocked down by tail

Big and small

Dinosaurs came in many different sizes. Some were enormous—much, much bigger than elephants. Some were small—no bigger than chickens—and there were all sizes in between.

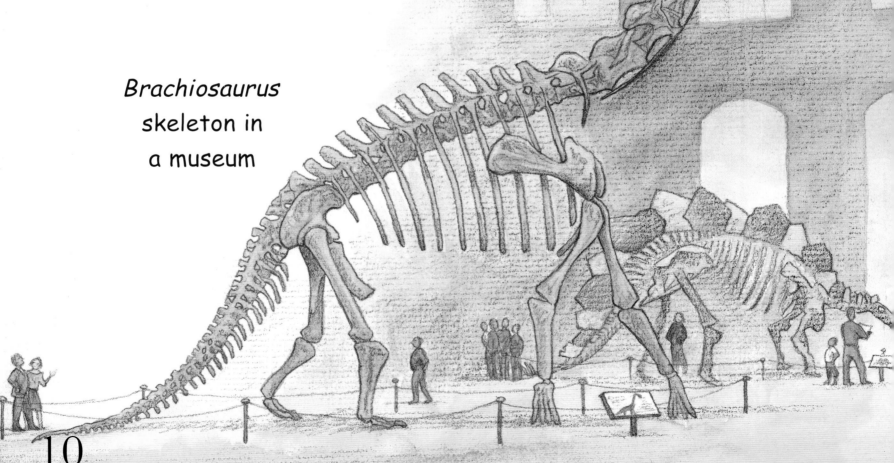

Brachiosaurus skeleton in a museum

1. What was the
biggest dinosaur?

2. Did dinosaurs
have big teeth?

3. What was the
smallest dinosaur?

1. The biggest plant-eating dinosaur that we know about is *Brachiosaurus*. It was 75 feet (23m) long and 39 feet (12m) high.

2. The meat eaters had big teeth. The plant eaters had small teeth, and the duck-billed dinosaurs had no teeth at all.

3. The smallest dinosaur we know about is *Compsognathus*, which was around the size of a crow.

Compsognathus skeleton

Dinosaur teeth

Allosaurus was a meat eater

big teeth

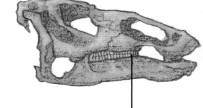

Edmontosaurus was a plant eater

small teeth

Struthiomimus was a duck-billed dinosaur

no teeth

Babies

Dinosaurs scraped nests out of earth or sand and laid eggs in them. Some covered the eggs in order to hide them and keep them warm. Some sat on their eggs, just like chickens and other birds do today.

Protoceratops on top of its nest

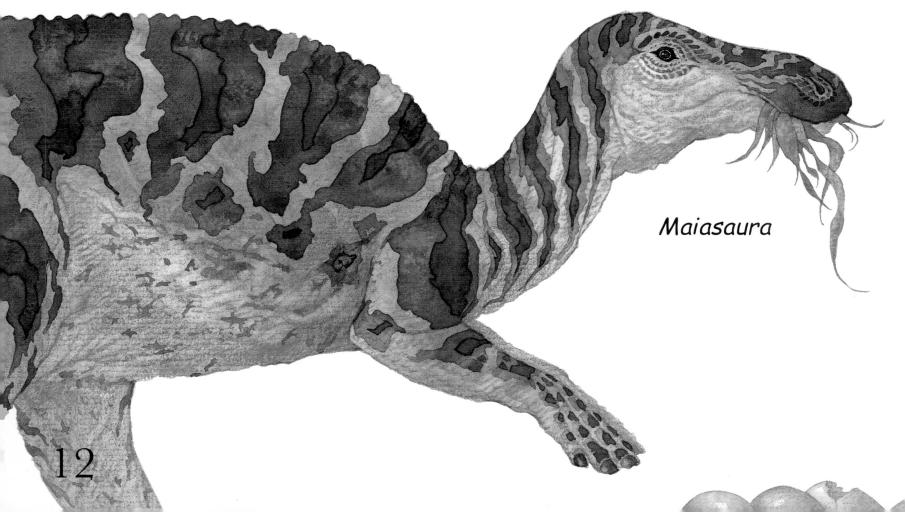

Maiasaura

12

1. Why didn't the eggs break when a dinosaur sat on them?

2. Did the dinosaurs help their babies get out of the eggs?

3. Did dinosaurs feed their babies?

eggs safe in
the nest

Maiasaura
feeding her
babies

1. Only small dinosaurs sat on their eggs. They weren't heavy enough to break them.

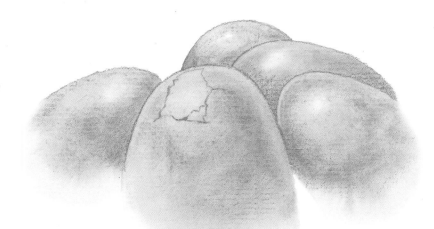

Psittacosaurus egg cracks and . . .

2. No. When they were ready, the babies broke out of the eggs themselves.

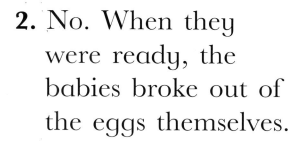

a head pops out!

3. Some dinosaurs, like the *Maiasaura*, fed their young. But some dinosaur babies had to find their own food.

The baby then breaks out of the egg.

13

What happened to the dinosaurs?

A huge asteroid crashed into Earth. There was a great explosion. Dust filled the air so that it was as dark as night. Huge waves and earthquakes shook the land. It was the end of the terrible lizards.

Edmontosaurus grazing

Dromaeosaur

1. What is an asteroid?

2. Did the asteroid kill all of the dinosaurs?

3. Are there any dinosaurs left?

asteroid hits
the ground

*Dromaeosaur
runs away*

1. An asteroid is a piece of rock that travels through space.

2. No, only some. Most of the dinosaurs were killed by earthquakes, drowned by huge waves, and choked by dust.

3. Yes. Some dinosaurs changed—over a very long time—into all of the birds that we see today.

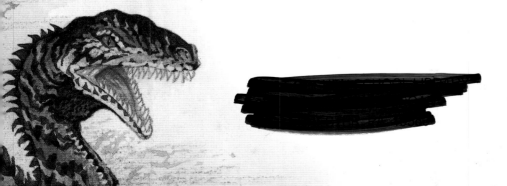

Changing from dinosaur to bird

Avimimus was a dinosaur that looked a little like a bird.

Archaeopteryx was the first bird. It lived with the dinosaurs.

Here are some birds that are alive today. 15

How do we know about dinosaurs?

Sometimes, when a dinosaur died, mud covered its body, and over millions of years it turned into a stone fossil. "Fossil" means "dug up," and a lot of fossil dinosaurs have been discovered.

Parasauralophus body lying in wet mud

paleontologists digging for fossils

16

1. What does a fossil dinosaur look like?

2. Who digs up the dinosaurs?

3. Has anything else been found?

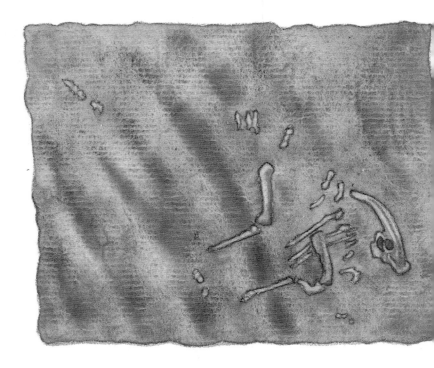

Parasauralophus skeleton
has turned into a fossil

a fossilized dinosaur
skeleton is uncovered

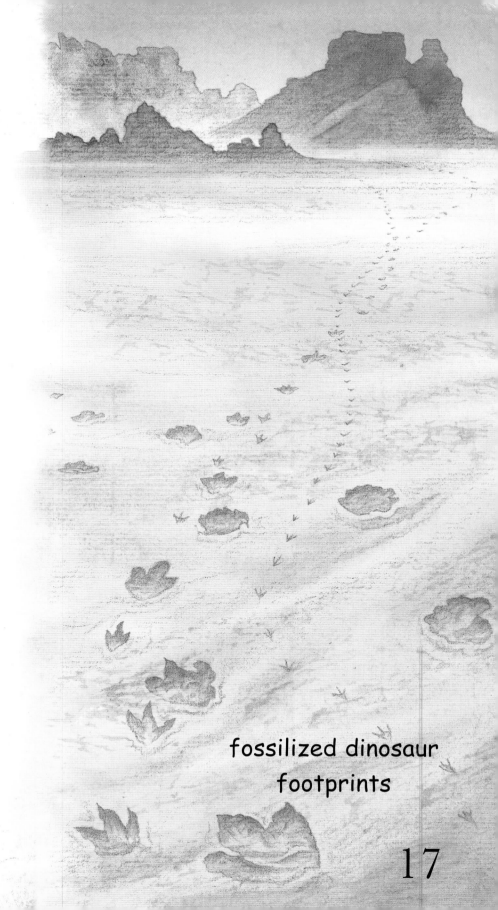

1. A fossil dinosaur looks like a skeleton. Sometimes only part of it is ever found.

2. Scientists who know a lot about fossils dig up dinosaurs. These scientists are called paleontologists ("pay-lee-on-toll-oh-jists").

3. Fossilized footprints have been found that show where dinosaurs walked.

fossilized dinosaur footprints

17

Index